MW01132432

Being a Bringer

Part 1 in the Bring | Teach | Keep Evangelism Series

Chuck Anderson & John Furness

Table of Contents

Foreword

Satan is a bonafide expert at pulling Christians away from their responsibility to take the Gospel to the world. The father of lies has used his timeless tools of fear, distraction, isolation, and persecution to convince the church that reaching lost souls is scary, demanding, and ultimately futile. Perhaps you have come to the conclusion that you have no role in evangelism, joining the countless number of Christians who have thrown up their hands in frustration and sighed, "I have tried and it just doesn't work for me." Or maybe you're anxious to get started, but a lack of confidence and preparation have left you scratching your head for answers. Take heart—God has prepared a role for every Christian in his congregation's evangelistic efforts. But to be successful, we must stop fighting against the devil's schemes according to our own wisdom. It is imperative that we understand and implement the Biblical model of evangelism, God's ordained method for growing the church.

The goal of the Bring Teach Keep ministry is to help congregations establish sustained growth by illuminating the Biblical model of evangelism and its 3 roles: Bringing, Teaching, and Keeping. The book you're reading now will provide insight into the role of the Bringer. It is so important to teach Christians with a talent for bringing how to improve their skills as they are truly at the frontline of the battlefield. It is also vital that Bringers understand how to work in harmony with Teachers and Keepers. Please seek out a copy of Bring Teach Keep: Illuminating the Biblical Model of Evangelism to understand how these 3 roles intertwine.

In this book, we'll discuss various topics including:

- The mission field.
- The mindset we need to develop.
- The mindset of seekers versus non-seekers.
- The responses we are likely to receive.
- The presence and role of Jesus in evangelism.
- The ability to love lost souls as Jesus did.
- The joy of leading others to Christ.
- Understanding that God is the one that gives increase.

Can you think of a time when all of these topics were discussed in relation to evangelism in a class or sermon series? I've heard them in bits and pieces but never in a single context where they could be understood together as a way to make us more effective in evangelism.

Above all else, we must always keep in mind that there is no book written by man that can totally encapsulate what it means to be a Bringer. Only the Bible can provide complete wisdom on the many facets of this role. When we truly begin to listen to Jesus and do things His way, it is then that He is able to providentially bless our efforts. God can and will bless the development of your skills as you incorporate bringing into your life according to His divine wisdom. May God bless you richly as you become more effective in evangelism!

~ Chuck Anderson

The Bringer Poster Child

Gerri was your average 16-year-old Christian girl—madly in love with her sweetheart, Joe. She knew that he wasn't a Christian, but that did not dilute her feelings for him in the slightest. They grew together as a couple and were married soon thereafter. In a short period of time, Joe enlisted in the army and was slated for duty in Germany. Unwilling to separate from each other, both Joe and Gerri set off to live abroad in an entirely foreign culture. This was the beginning of Gerri's separation from the Lord and His church, a departure that lasted nearly 40 years.

Many years later, back in America, Gerri was moved to attend a worship service with her daughter and four granddaughters. She came forward that Sunday morning, confessed her absence, and asked to be welcomed back into fellowship with the church. Of course, her request was granted with great enthusiasm! When I got the chance to personally meet her after service, I offered to conduct a "Bible timeline" study in her home, and she graciously accepted. Gerri continued to seek the Lord daily and grew in love for Him and for the church. Her soul was once again secure—a resounding success! But that's far from the end of the story. No one was prepared for what happened next.

Full of zeal for Christ, Gerri reached out to countless friends and family members, bringing over 100 people either to worship or a Bible study in just three years time. She gently led her husband Joe to faith, and he has since become a force to be reckoned with, writing sermons and participating in worship and service. The couple have helped the church throughout northern Michigan by using their land for church functions, including a teen Gospel meeting where over 75 people participated in community service and outreach.

Gerri is an incredible proof of the power of God working in someone's life. She isn't a trained preacher, a Biblical scholar, or an evangelist, but one willing soul who said, "I am going to do all that I can with what God has given me." To this day, Gerri openly admits that she is not a teacher. She continues to use her amazing gift to bring others into contact with those who can teach. This illustrates the metaphor of the church as Christ's body so beautifully. In evangelism, some were designed to be hands and others were created as mouths. Every member has a unique function.

But there's a twist in Gerri's story that I haven't yet mentioned. You see, her recommitment to the Lord nearly died right in the church parking lot the day she decided to return. As she tells the tale, she literally put one foot out of the van then pulled it back in, second guessing her decision to recommit. I think that moment so accurately represents where many Christians are regarding evangelism. They have the desire to go forward but, when the time comes to act, shrivel back in fear. I truly believe that most Christians want to be evangelistic. Unfortunately, they don't know where they belong or how they've been gifted.

As I understand the "Great Commission" from Matthew 28:18-20, evangelism involves 3 areas of activity:

All authority has been given to me in heaven and on earth. Go [Bring] therefore and make disciples [Teach] of all nations, baptizing them in the name of the Father, and of the Son and of the Holy Spirit, teaching them to observe all that I have commanded you [Keep] and lo, I am with you even to the end of the age.

Each Christian has been gifted in some way to fulfill the role associated with one or more of these areas.

Bringers: These are Christians who have a talent for inviting people to come to worship, a Gospel meeting, a Bible study or some event where they can be exposed to Jesus and His people. They may not be especially eloquent or educated but have the desire to see all saved and are willing to reach out.

Teachers: These are Christians who can guide a lost soul through the Bible and answer his questions well enough to lead him to obedience. They are equipped to lay out the plan of salvation in a clear and scriptural manner.

Keepers: These are Christians who work to retain other Christians, primarily those who have just given their lives to the Lord and are growing in the faith. The role of the Brother's Keeper is the "forgotten" facet of our evangelistic efforts.

From my experience in presenting seminars and talking with Christians around the country, I've learned that most do not have a basic understanding of this breakdown of roles and separation of duties. More often than not, we send new converts out to teach the Gospel to their family, friends, and neighbors without really considering the implication that we are pegging everyone as a teacher.

This approach clearly contradicts two passages of Scripture.

> Not many of you should become teachers, my brothers, for you know that we who teach will be judged with greater strictness (James 3:1).

According to James, not everyone in the congregation is a teacher. In fact, few should pursue this role. When we push untrained or unwilling members into a teaching role, we place them in a situation where they will be judged more strictly. In addition, we may completely douse their fire for evangelism by forcing them to teach when they may instead be gifted as a Bringer or Keeper.

> Now you are the body of Christ and individually members of it. And God has appointed in the church first Apostles, second prophets, third teachers, then miracles, then gifts of healing, helping, administrating and various kinds of tongues. Are all Apostles? Are all prophets? Are all teachers? Do all work miracles? Do all possess gifts of healing? Do all speak with tongues? Do all interpret (1 Corinthians 12:27-30)?

The beautiful metaphor of the church being identified as a body emphasizes that all of us do not have the same gifts and abilities. Here, Paul asks a series of rhetorical questions that would obviously receive a "no" answer. It is very apparent that the Holy Spirit does not believe we are all fit to teach.

It needs to be clarified that I am speaking of a teacher in the context of evangelism. In other words, I am identifying the act of being skilled enough to lead someone to Jesus using scripture. Surely, our daily example to the world is critical, but this will not teach anybody what they must do to be saved. We cannot teach the path to salvation through our actions alone. We must present the truth as found in God's word.

In the following chapters, we'll examine some challenges to the work of the Bringer and also present some Biblical solutions. As you read on, try to envision yourself in this evangelistic role to see if it might be a good fit for you. The Kingdom needs a strong force of trained Bringers who understand the urgency and gravity of the job. Souls hang in the balance!

Who Will Listen

If you could be the proverbial "fly on the wall" during my first 5 years as a Christian, you would see the principle of misdirected enthusiasm in full force. I was unhindered with zeal for the Lord, wanting so badly for my friends and family to accept the Gospel. I convinced myself that I was going to almost effortlessly change the lives of everyone I knew or came in contact with. Obviously, I hadn't given much thought to Matthew 7:13-14, where Jesus says that "the gate is narrow and the way is hard that leads to life and those who find it are few." I was never taught that most people would reject my offer to study the Bible. My skewed understanding of evangelism, coupled with unrealistic expectations, ultimately led to a lot of heartache and discouragement. Thankfully, my father-in-law stepped in and offered counsel that, while hard to receive, was critical to my growth. Most distinctly, I remember him saying, "The first 5 years I was a Christian, I repelled more people than I attracted." I realized I was doing the very same thing.

SAD STATISTICS

As I speak at seminars around the country, I am astounded by the lack of awareness Christians have of the negative undercurrent Satan is stirring up beneath us. The following statistics from the November 2016 issue of "Think" magazine illustrate the degree to which the church of Christ is declining:

- A recent "Pew Research" poll showed that "nones" (those with no religious affiliation) are on the rise, up from 16% of the population in 2007 to 23% in 2015.
- 70% of young adults born from 1990–1996 with no religious affiliation say that religion is not important in their lives and 42% say they do not believe in God.
- On average, a congregation in the United States reaches its highest attendance by its 30th year in existence then begins to decline in number.

There is overwhelming evidence that the influence of the Bible in the United States has diminished. It would be easy to shrink into a mindset of futility; however, it is critical that we use such information to inspire zeal for the mission at hand. Given these trends, the big picture may look bleak, but every Christian has an important role in the local congregation. If every faithful child of God put a hand to the plow according to his unique talents, we could correct the atrophy, one soul at a time.

To the reader who wants to become a better bringer, the Bible offers a sizable amount of information about the world we are called to engage. Always remember that we are pilgrims passing through an alien land with an eternal citizenship in Heaven. We operate in a way foreign to those devoted to this world. We understand things that are spiritually sent because we have the Spirit of Christ; the world cannot understand them because they are "spiritually discerned" (1 Corinthians 2:14). The best advice I can give you at the beginning of your journey is to pray to our Father about the ministry into which you are "stepping your foot out of the van."

Ask for help in loving the lost. I suggest that you keep in mind the first few verses of 1 Corinthians 13. It isn't about results, but about loving souls enough to allow God to work through you, even when it seems that no one is listening.

Biblical Understanding That Empowers Bringers

Evangelism is often treated as a tricky task, something to be left to those who are smarter or more confident. However, the truth is that there is no special formula or perfect candidate. The Bible communicates all that we need to know to be effective so that any Christian can be a force for good in evangelism. This chapter sets the tone for the rest of the material by using Scripture to identify three components of the Biblical model for bringing:

The Individual - How Jesus refers to each Christian.
The Territory - What Jesus is sending us out into.
The Wisdom - What we need to know to navigate the territory.

THE INDIVIDUAL

The key to becoming mature in Christ and effective in evangelism is to cultivate a genuine heart of love. Consider 1 Corinthians 13. Often referred to as the "love chapter," it is here that Paul describes a number of spectacular actions—speaking in tongues, prophesying, understanding all mysteries, faith strong enough to move mountains—that mean absolutely nothing in the eternal scheme if not performed with love. Jesus himself, when asked about the greatest commandment, responded:

> You shall love the Lord your God with all your heart and with all your soul and with all your mind. This is the great and first commandment. And a second is like it: You shall love your neighbor as yourself. On these two commandments depend all the Law and the Prophets (Matthew 22:37-40).

Without love, the law and prophets are completely undermined. They simply cease to make sense. They lose their power. Our God, who is love incarnate, dictates that we focus our efforts on others through a heart of love in order to accomplish His will. He requires we love Him first and then others as we love ourselves.

Once we understand that evangelism thrives only when rooted in love, we can better understand some of the illustrations that Jesus uses to describe the role of the bringer. In Matthew 9:36-38, Jesus identifies us as laborers: "When he saw the crowds, he had compassion for them, because they were harassed and helpless, like sheep without a shepherd. Then he said to his disciples, 'The harvest is plentiful, but the laborers are few; therefore pray earnestly to the Lord of the harvest to send out laborers into his harvest.'" Here, Jesus shows compassion toward a lost, shepherd-less people. As His laborers, we must have the same heart and work ethic toward those who might be seeking. We must recognize His authority, listen to His command, and fulfill our duty, just as an employee respects and responds to his employer.

The Savior highlights a complementary side of the bringer role in Matthew 10:16. In this passage, He identifies us as sheep, defenseless, and dependent. Sheep are in total need of the shepherd's guidance and protection. This helps us understand how important it is to "listen to His voice." It also clarifies that Jesus knows us personally, so He can advise us on how we ought to behave as the flock of His pasture.

THE TERRITORY

The territory is the space we must navigate while looking for seeking souls. You may be envisioning a physical location, like your school or the grocery store, and while that is certainly part of the picture, I want you to understand that the true territory, the place where the battle actually takes place, is the mind of the hearer. If we are to successfully reach out to others, we must distinguish between these two planes. Paul said in Ephesians 6:12 that "our battle is not against flesh and blood" but against the powers of darkness that influence the mind of the hearer. It's so easy to react to the hearer in such a way that leads us to get angry at him and not at the source of his thoughts. Remember that the hearer who rejects your offer is unable to defeat the powers of darkness on his own. Like you and I, he needs the power of God in his life to affect that kind of change. Do you see how understanding this helps us to look with compassion instead of spite? I find it so much easier to be effective when my heart isn't devising a vengeful comment but is trying to make the environment as rich as possible for the hearer so that he comes back to me in the future to hear the word in it's powerful, freeing simplicity.

Think about the way Jesus dealt with rejection. He knew the rich young ruler would walk away, yet He looked on him with love (Matthew 19:16-22). He loved those Jews who rejected Him as a mother hen does her chicks (Matthew 23:37). When they hung Him on the cruel cross of Calvary, he prayed, "Father, forgive them for they know not what they do" (Luke 23:34). Ponder the depth of love that hopes for the best for those who persecute. Jesus give us an astounding example of how we need to have pity upon those who persecute us because they are under the control of Satan. Through experience, we deepen our respect and awe of what Jesus went through and become stronger and more able to handle the types of people that we will encounter in the world.

Visualizing the Territory

In the picture above, the church is surrounded by numerous instances of the letter "S," which represent true seekers of God around you. These could be those in the literal proximity of the church building or those whom you come in contact with as you travel through your day. Most often, this is the type of image that we have in mind when we think about the mission field. But this is not the whole picture. The situation is not so cut-and-dry.

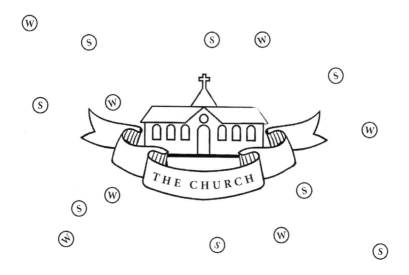

Jesus says that He is sending us out as sheep amongst wolves. It is not hard to imagine what happens to a sheep who encounters a wolf without some sort of intervention. As the literal sheep is in need of a shepherd to guide, protect and save it from danger, we also need to arm and guard ourselves using the guidance of our Shepherd, Jesus. I find this analogy fascinating. Sheep do not possess the protective means that we humans have—knives, guns, vehicles, or a cunning intellect. The Lord asks us to picture ourselves as sheep to understand the true danger of venturing out into the territory alone. In the absence of its shepherd, a sheep is easy prey for even a lone wolf.

Psalm 23:5 reinforces the necessity of our reliance on Jesus as we seek lost souls. The psalmist writes, "You prepare my table in the presence of my enemies." Notice that David didn't say "You remove my enemies from my presence." Even when we are surrounded by enemies, He still prepares our table. He provides for us sustenance, protection, and guidance, as long as we abide in Him.

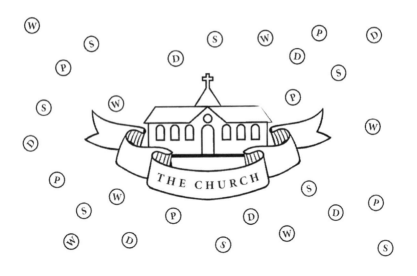

Jesus uses two more animals in Matthew 7:6 to depict the nature and character of those Satan uses to oppose us as we evangelize: dogs and pigs. In the image above, these are represented by the "D's" and "P's."

To the Jews of Jesus' day, dogs and pigs were considered squalid, unclean, scavengers. We should not picture them as little puppies or pet pigs, but as vicious, feral and destructive. I once had the opportunity to observe a penned-up feral hog on the property of a Christian brother in northern Michigan. The animal was amazingly huge, weighing at least 500 pounds, yet at first glance, it appeared rather harmless as it slept behind the strong fencing. I asked if I could reach in and pet it and he promptly told me, "Sure… once!" His point was that although it appeared docile, it was waiting for a chance to strike out. Likewise, there are those in the world waiting for the opportunity to spiritually maim the children of God. Jesus is clearly telling us here that there are those who would desire our destruction.

Next, we see an even more troubling enemy, who isn't usually regarded as a threat to our life. These are the non-seekers, represented by the N's in the picture above. They are so dangerous to our mission because they do not outright intend to do us harm. Instead, they blend in more easily with the true seekers and can ensnare us if we are not discerning.

In 2 Corinthians 11:14, the Holy Spirit gives an invaluable insight regarding non-seekers. Paul writes that "even Satan transforms himself into an angel of light." In the world, there are millions of wonderful people who exist outside the body of Christ. Their lives are marked by acts of kindness and consideration toward others, and they make a positive impact on the community. Because they are viewed so highly, we often tend to excuse or look past the fact that they have never accepted God on His terms. This is the toughest part for many to deal with. Always remember that there is no level of kindness or moral aptitude that man can achieve to forgive sin. The only element powerful enough to save man is the blood of Christ, which in turn is applied only to those who obey the Gospel. Therefore, great care needs to be taken to ensure that we do not pervert the New Testament plan of salvation as delivered by the Holy Spirit in order to maintain a friendly relationship with the many sweet yet unsaved people that we know.

Satan will attempt to darken our thoughts in this manner by convincing us that faulty doctrine is acceptable because of the kindness of the person teaching it. This is a deathtrap in the strongest sense of the phrase because the consequences are eternal. Jesus said in John 14:6, "I am the way and the truth and the life and no man comes to the Father but through Me." When we compromise the Biblical plan of salvation in order to cater to a friend's feelings or avoid conflict with a pleasant neighbor, we abandon this foundation of truth and call the Savior a liar. To clarify, not many of the "N's" in the world are out to destroy us—they are friends, neighbors, co-workers and teammates. That's why this demographic is so difficult to handle!

I hope you can see that the territory is varied and challenging. There are those who will blatantly try to destroy us, while others may confuse our mission by presenting themselves as "good" people. No wonder we so often become silent. Nonetheless, we must be vigilant to also understand the group of people who drive us to continue on our evangelistic mission.

Notice the stark difference between the common perception of the territory (top) and the reality of the situation (bottom).

Seekers

I place special emphasis on this group because these are the target of our whole mission. As we offer the Gospel to everyone, we will find out that most belong to one of the first 4 groups: wolves, dogs, pigs and good people outside of Christ. How beautiful it is then when we endure long enough to find a seeker. It truly makes all of the rejection fade into insignificance!

I was blessed to be a part of an annual meeting with a congregation in Alabama where the theme of "bring, teach, keep" was being planned. In the outreach meeting, I was asked a very pertinent question: "How do you identify a seeker?" This is evangelism 101. If we can identify a seeker, it makes it vividly clear who the non-seekers are. Simply put, we identify them by their actions and reactions to our Gospel offer. Our discussion led us to the fact that seekers are active. They don't always know what (or more importantly, Whom) they're seeking; they just know things are not right with their lives.

This is important to know so we can be patient with them. Our conversation made me think of my own conversion. I waited two years to finally ask Paul Schandevel, my Christian co-worker, why he lived so differently than anyone else I knew. I personally believed in God, so I thought that couldn't have been the key factor. I considered the possibility that it was a different job, a different location, or the fact that he was married. I was seeking the path to a better life but had no idea it was the one whom I had eliminated from the start—Jesus Christ! This makes so much sense to me now. Paul's shining light was his relationship with the Father, and it was so attractive that it moved me to desire that for my own life.

We must also be mindful that some are actively seeking, but not for "the Kingdom of God and His righteousness." I have run into people who were looking for warm and fuzzy religious conversations, an avenue to show their value, or an opportunity to brag about themselves—basically, anything other than true conversion. Be careful of these because they will continually waste your time and energy. When they fail to obey the Gospel, we usually place the guilt back on ourselves even though they weren't truly seeking in the first place.

There are many other passages that shed light on the distinction between non-seekers and seekers including John 10:27, Galatians 4:16, Matthew 15:9, and Matthew 6:33, to name a few. However, for now let's discuss some passages that inform us how to navigate the territory while avoiding discouragement.

THE WISDOM

In Colossians 4:5-6, Paul gives us instruction on how to navigate the territory we just wrote about: "Walk in wisdom towards outsiders, making the best use of your time. Let your speech always be gracious, seasoned with salt, so you may know how to answer each person." Take note of two very powerful pieces of wisdom. First, he instructs us to be wise, which undoubtedly is telling us to pray for wisdom ourselves. He then tells us how to speak, not what to say. Often, the way we say something carries more weight to the hearer than the actual words themselves. Salt-seasoned words are a surprising oddity compared to the world's way of communicating. When we speak graciously, we develop a characteristic that draws people to us.

I'm often asked, "What do you say to someone to open up the conversation about the Gospel?" Immediately, I know that this brother or sister is asking a question out of total sincerity, yet it also tells me there is a huge misunderstanding of evangelism which is answered in these two verses. Since each person is different, I refrain from giving them an "opening line," and instead refer them to these verses to give them a far greater piece of wisdom. The Holy Spirit inspired Paul to give us the main focus of our approach: gracious, salt-seasoned speech out of a heart of love. This must be the foundation of how we approach every single person. When this love begins in our heart, it is so much easier for us to find the words to say. It also guides us (along with prayer and Bible study) to determine the right time to speak and what to say.

Shaking the Dust From Our Feet

In the times of the Bible, washing a traveler's feet was a respectful practice that honored visitors who came into one's home, as it rid guests of the filth that clung to their feet from their journey. In Matthew 10:12-14, Jesus uses this analogy to give us wisdom pertaining to evangelism. He says to "shake the dust off your feet" if a house or city doesn't receive you. The parallel here is to make sure we don't let negativity—the dirt of the ground—cling to us as we move past rejection. In other words, do not let their rejection of the greatest gift to mankind deter you. Shake it off and continue to search for a seeker.

Keeping Ourselves Pure

As we reach out to the world, we can expect to encounter those with proverbially "unwashed feet." Those outside of Christ will naturally manifest unspiritual behaviors. However, while doing so, we must be careful not to develop close relationships with those who reject the Gospel to the extent that it erodes our own faith. This does not mean we don't have good relationships with lost souls. It means to be very careful that we don't slowly slip into their ways. The danger is that it happens so subtly. I know of many families in the church that have fostered closer relationships with those in the world than with other brethren, and left the church for other denominations. Countless horror stories are told of children who have gone off to college and lost their faith.

In 1 Corinthians 15:33, we are told that "evil companionships corrupt good morals." The word "corrupt" in the Greek is "ptheiro," which means to whither, spoil, or shrivel. These are words that express a slow process as opposed to an instantaneous occurrence. Because of this slow process, it is often difficult to detect when we are slipping. As we nurture worldly companionships, we place ourselves in danger of shriveling the goodness we have developed in Jesus.

Wise as Serpents, Gentle as Doves

In Matthew 10:16, Jesus tells His followers, "I am sending you out as sheep in the midst of wolves, so be wise as serpents and innocent as doves." The Lord indicates that we are not to approach evangelism like a propagandist, indiscriminately dropping leaflets into enemy territory. Instead, we must approach the mission like a vulnerable soldier infiltrating the enemy line. Our job requires forethought and tact in order to both minimize casualties and maximize returns. In Jesus' counsel to us, he describes two characteristics that we should adopt in order to protect us as we search out seekers.

Firstly, we must be wise as serpents. The image of a serpent typically suggests evil intention, but that is certainly not the characteristic that Jesus wants us to emulate here. Instead, he uses the image of a snake to represent a discerning quality that we can hone for good. The Lord's desire is for us to draw as many true seekers out from among the ranks of the wolves as possible. Surely, a healthy dose of God's wisdom will be a benefit to our efforts.

Secondly, we must be innocent as doves. Here, the Greek word for "innocent" is "akeraios," which when translated means "unmixed." As we enter the wolf pack, it is imperative that we maintain a Biblical foundation and not adopt a worldly way of thinking. For example, the world tells us that simply being a good person should be enough to warrant Heaven, but this kind of thinking is absolutely detrimental to Biblical evangelism. We know that not all "good people" go to Heaven—it is only by the blood of Christ that sinners receive God's mercy. Jesus counsels us to remain unmixed so that our evangelistic efforts bring souls to Christ, not just to comfort.

Lessons from the Unjust Steward

In Luke 16:1-13, Jesus tells the parable of the unjust steward. In this story, the steward makes provisions by worldly means to ensure that he has financial security after being fired. Jesus does not praise his evil, but rather states that if the children of light were as wise in spiritual things as the evil man was in evil things, they would be preparing well for Heaven. The whole point being made here is that there must be some logical, systematic way to take the Gospel to the world. This is not something that we thoughtlessly "go and do," but a task that we are called to approach with forethought and discernment. In other words, like the steward, we need an end-game plan. As a bringer, this would involve thinking about, praying for, and loving those we reach out to so that we can take advantage of the moments when the seeker is most receptive.

Not Seeing the Forest for the Trees

As we reach out to people, it's common to begin the journey with both great intentions and unrealistic expectations. Far too often, after a series of "no" answers, Satan puts thoughts in our head about how unsuccessful we are. He distracts us from the truth by hiding it from our minds. We can look back to Genesis where the Devil approached Eve as she stood near the tree of knowledge of good and evil. The first thing he did was eliminate the idea of God as "Lord," reducing the loving, covenant God to "the big powerful one who cheated Eve." Then Satan removed the thought of all the food God had blessed them to eat and isolated her attention to the trees. Why? Because the "evil" act would only be in effect if they ate from the tree of knowledge of good and evil. No need to explain where this led!

The same thing happens to us when we receive rejection. Jesus said in Matthew 7:13-14 that most will take the wide path to destruction and few will choose to take the narrow path that leads to life. Simply put, most people we encounter will not obey the Gospel. But Satan tells us to forget about the other vegetation and focus on just the trees. He wants us consumed by the "no" answers (the trees) so that we forget about the seekers we are after (the good vegetation all around us). Do you see that the guilt we place on ourselves over rejection is not from God? Instead, imagine God telling you, "Thank you for continuing to do My will. In My eyes you are an absolute success. Shake the dust off of your feet and find those seeking Me. I will lead them across your path."

"No" is Not a Bad Answer

A lack of evangelism training in the church has made it so easy for Satan to stunt our growth using his favorite go-to tool: the fear of rejection. Think about how effective it is. Not only does it prevent a lost soul from hearing the life-changing Gospel, but it also renders a potential all-star evangelist defunct, killing two birds with one stone. But would you be surprised if I told you that receiving rejection is not always bad? In fact, sometimes it's the desired response to our outreach. If the church could collectively wrap its head around this principle, it would be an unstoppable soul-saving force. Here are a few reasons why "no" is often a positive response to our efforts.

REASON 1: YOU HAVE PLEASED GOD.

What greater accomplishment can a Christian acheive than pleasing God? Truly, nothing else matters. As you venture into your role as a bringer, never forget this foundational truth. By doing our part to bring His plan of salvation to completion in our time, we can begin to comprehend the deep, inner joy of knowing that our actions cause a smile to spread across the face of almighty God.

Granted, it can be hard when your efforts produce a seemingly insurmountable mountain of rejection. Is God pleased with evangelism that seems to bear no fruit? It's important to remember that even Jesus, the master evangelist, failed to convert many of the people with whom He spoke. There was no issue with the effectiveness of His method or the power of His message, but rather with the hardened hearts of the people He sought to save. In John 8:29, Jesus said that He always does the things that please His Father. As we reach out to lost souls, even those who reject the Gospel, we walk in the footsteps of the Savior.

REASON 2: GOD'S WORD DID NOT RETURN VOID.

Does a sincere offer to study or worship ever really return void? The normal response of the Christian is to analyze the situation saying, "If only I had offered it differently or more eloquently." The real problem with this is that we are saying that "we" are the power! We need to remember that there are three parties involved in evangelism:

Me / The Hearer(s) / God

Each of these parties operate independently and cannot supersede the free will of the other two. When we take rejection personally, we overstep the boundaries of our area and try to take the reigns from God. Remember Paul's words in 1 Corinthians 3:7—he and Apollos planted and watered but God gave the increase. If we offer the Gospel to someone in a kind, loving manner and they reject the offer, it is like the scattered seed from Jesus' famed parable that fell on hard soil. There was no lack of power in the seed. Rather, the seed was not allowed to unleash its power due to an infertile landscape. God does not sleep, nor does He fail to acknowledge and bless a seeker (2 Peter 3:9).

REASON 3: YOU HAVE IDENTIFIED YOURSELF AS THE PLACE THEY SHOULD GO TO SEEK.

When your offer is rejected, console yourself with the idea that you have identified yourself as a source of Bible knowledge in another person's life. Should they decide to seek truth in the future, perhaps you will be the one they turn to for answers. The key is to be patient as you attempt to bring people. Like Gerri, they may not look again for 40 years.

Of course, their perception of Christianity will be strongly flavored by the way you treat them. The chances of them returning are contingent upon your attitude and approach. If upon receiving a "no," we force the conversation to continue against their wishes, we are beginning to build a wall between us and them. Treat them nicely, accept their answer, and gently let them know that they can seek you out if they ever change their mind.

A farmer prepares the soil before sowing. The soil is the heart of the believer, and we plant and water together. We do not grant the increase. God does. By being kind to those who respond to us with a "no," we are prepping the soil so our God is able to grant the increase. If we are not kind, we are making that soil less fertile for growth now and later.

REASON 4: THE PERSON IS NOT CURRENTLY SEEKING.

"Seek and you shall find" is an eternal truth from the throne of God that is so simple to understand, yet like most things, we complicate it with human wisdom. In my years as an evangelist, I've heard many brethren say with conviction, "I have asked my non-Christian spouse to worship every Sunday for years and will continue to do so until I die." Really? Did it not occur to this person that their spouse received the offer, considered it every week for many years, and continued to say "no?" The logical conclusion would be that the spouse is not seeking, therefore he cannot find.

One of the best examples to learn from is Jesus' encounter with the rich young ruler. In Mark 10:22, the Lord tells the young man to sell his goods, give them to the poor, and come follow Him. As we know, the clear command was understood by the recipient and rejected. The key here is that Jesus let him walk away. He did not offer a lesser responsibility or negotiate conditions. He did not beg him to reconsider on the spot. Jesus allowed the man to reject His offer and went on to find the next potential seeker.

In his letter to the church in Corinth, Paul addressed the differences between the the natural man (non-seeker) and the spiritual man (faithful Christian). Paul writes very plainly that the natural man cannot understand the things of God because they are folly to him, "for the things of God are spiritually discerned." Imagine trying to convince a man to carry an unborn child within himself for 9 months. We can beg, threaten, and guilt the husband, but regardless of our attempts, it is simply an impossibility. The same is true when we beg, threaten, and guilt non-seekers. As the husband cannot carry a child, neither can the natural man hear spiritual things. We must accept rejection kindly and pray for a day when the hearer will be ready to appeal to spiritual reasoning.

REASON 5: YOUR OFFER WAS HEARD, CONSIDERED AND REJECTED.

If you were to offer a crisp $100 bill to a random person on the street, but you did so with a spirit of harshness, how many do you think would take it? In my mind, at least 95% would accept the money despite your attitude toward them because of the value of the offer. Now imagine a scenario where you kindly offer the gospel, but are told "no." Did the potential recipient reject you personally, or did they reject the offer? Of course, it was the gospel that they rejected because they place no value on the offer.

People accept things that they believe will help them based on prior knowledge. The usefulness of money is something we are all aware of, so it would come as no surprise that a stranger would accept a free $100 bill. The Gospel, however, is quite different because people have preconceived notions about it. They may have encountered a Christian who tried to force the Bible upon them or visited a congregation that treated them poorly, and now they have a skewed perception of the church as a whole. A false preacher on television, teaching on atheistic evolution, or confusion over denominational division may have devalued the Gospel in their eyes. As you look for true seekers, strive to convey the unparalleled value of the gospel to non-seekers. If they ever begin to seek and you initially approached them in kindness and grace, you may very well be the one they remember and turn to.

REASON 6: THEY CANNOT SAY GOD NEVER SENT ANYONE TO WARN THEM.

The first few chapters of Ezekiel contain a profound look at God's desire to rescue souls, even those who strongly oppose Him. Ezekiel, who had been taken captive with many of his Hebrew brethren in Babylon, received a bizarre vision from God followed by clear instruction to take a message of warning to his countrymen. Yet, even more striking than the vision itself was God's reflection on the hearts of His people, when He said to Ezekiel that "the house of Israel will not be willing to listen to you" (Ezekiel 3:7). His own people, descendants of faithful Abraham, had turned their backs on Him, but God still went above and beyond so that no one could accuse Him at the judgment with the words "you never warned us." This is exactly how we must treat those who have turned their back on God today. We need to share the Gospel with courage and respect, knowing that every single person that tells you "no" is in the same position as those who rejected God's message from Ezekiel. They have been warned and will not face God unaccountable.

Capacities of the Bringer

When I first became a Christian, I was so enamored by a certain brother that I tried to imitate him in every way, even to the point of changing the inflection of my voice as I rattled off his favorite one-liners. I wanted to be his clone. As I matured, however, I realized that this was not a healthy pursuit. What I should have done is adopt his Godly behaviors while becoming the best Chuck I could be. Unknowingly, I was telling God that he made a mistake when he made me.

This can happen to us in evangelism if we're not careful. We see brethren who seem to evangelize almost flawlessly, as if they were born with the innate ability to convert others to Christ. But this is so far from true. Every Christian has gone through a similar process of growth and refinement—from the early stages as a babe in Christ, to childhood where they discover their talents, to adolescence where they develop their talents further and begin to step out on their own, to maturity where they engage others while continuing to grow.

Here is where the metaphor of the church as a body is so important. Every body part is required for the whole body to function at full capacity, but not all parts work the same. In fact, there are many separate parts that do the same thing to a large degree, like tendons and ligaments, yet there are very major differences in their capacities. The strong tendons and ligaments in my legs that allow me to run have much more capacity than those in my fingers. While they operate in very similar ways, far less is required of some than others. The same is true of the members of the body of Christ.

Earlier I talked about Gerri, who has been wonderfully successful in her work since she decided to "put her foot out of the van." If you are a female Gerri's age, you may feel required to match her efficiency in reaching out to others. But replicating Gerri is not our command. Instead, we must do the best with what God has made us to be.

Can you or I precisely emulate Gerri anyway? Consider the many factors that contributed to her unique situation:

1. Do you have the identical background?
2. Do you have the same personality?
3. Do you have the same motivation?
4. Are you in the same culture and sphere of influence?
5. Are your contacts the same in number?
6. Do you have someone guiding you with Biblical wisdom?
7. Do you have the same support systems (family, church)?

It is wonderful to try to imitate those we admire and respect, but we need to take care not to compare our output with anybody else's. Remember that God always grants the increase.

EVANGELISM IS NOT A COMPETITION.

Do not judge your own development or success as a bringer by anything other than Scripture and the unique providence God blesses you with. Others may be outspoken, knocking doors and talking to folks they have never met, but this does not mean that you must do the same. This would be a huge burden to someone who is introverted or shy. In fact, it would most likely shut them down the same way a non-teacher is discouraged when told they must teach. We need to recognize these traits in ourselves and move towards developing ourselves where we are most effective, instead of continually comparing ourselves to others.

GOD WILL DEVELOP YOUR UNIQUE ABILITIES.

I am persuaded that just as the world is full of diverse personalities, so is the church. Therefore, for us to be able to connect with those outside the church, it makes sense that the same diversity must be present inside the church. Don't try to change who you are because you see someone else bringing more people than you; it is God who is granting the increase, not them or you. It's natural and healthy to seek counsel from each other to help fine-tune our efforts, but do not try to become someone else.

Satan knows very well the territory we are being sent into. One of his tactics is to convince us that we are not equipped for evangelism because we are not like this brother or that sister. When convinced of this, we are saying that God didn't equip us properly for the task He has given. The only tool Satan has is founded on lies, so don't let him have this one—you are definitely equipped to accomplish the task God has given you. You may not like it, it may be tough in the beginning, and you may lose friends or create friction with people in your life. We are told that this is going to occur to some degree or another, so don't believe you are doing wrong when it happens. Reflect on what happened to Jesus. Your goal is to become the best "you," and that is done by becoming like Jesus.

YOU DO NOT NEED A BIBLE DEGREE TO BE AN EFFECTIVE BRINGER.

Bringing is a considerably different challenge than teaching or keeping. Teachers must have considerable Bible knowledge and experience to move throughout the Scriptures to answer questions and lead people. Keepers must have some life experience in the church to help the new Christian be able to deal with issues they encounter. On the flipside, the most effective bringers, in my experience, are the newly converted because they are so excited about their new faith. The thrill of having their sins washed away is still very fresh, and Satan hasn't had time to dull its luster. The big difference isn't a Bible degree, years of experience, or extensive training, but the heart and excitement of their pearl being so shiny and beautifully created (Matthew 13:45-46).

ALL OF US HAVE DIFFERENT CIRCLES OF PEOPLE.

We all travel different paths and find ourselves mixed amongst different circles of people. Some Christians are employed where they intersect with many new people each week, while others interact with the same few day in and day out. No matter where we find ourselves, God is aware of our unique situation as well as the hearts of those around us. It is our responsibility to do what we can to produce a desire to seek in others.

Don't look at a sister who is bringing many people and conclude you are failing because your numbers don't compare. Remember the parable of the one and five talent individuals in the Bible. God was well aware that the five talent person was given five talents and He required only five in return—not four and not six. Likewise, if there is no one around you that is seeking at this present time, God will not require you to squeeze a seeker out of a non-seeker.

DON'T TOTALLY CONSUME YOURSELF WITH BRINGING THAT YOU OMIT OTHER AREAS OF LIFE.

Evangelism is something that is best accomplished when we incorporate it into our daily lives along with the other responsibilities we have been given. It would be so wrong of a mother of small children to neglect her duty as a mother to knock doors every day. On the other hand, it would be very wise for her to use her children as an opportunity to reach out to people. As she walks with her children, she can praise them in front of those that she meets. She can mention their excitement for the upcoming VBS or the youth group functions they're involved in. She does not abandon her children for evangelism but uses them as an opportunity. We should examine our lives to see what we have that can be used in a similar manner.

Peace in Evangelism That Passes Understanding

"Do not be anxious about anything, but in everything by prayer and supplication with thanksgiving let your requests be made known to God. And the peace of God, which surpasses all understanding, will guard your hearts and your minds in Christ Jesus" (Philippians 4:6-7).

One of the biggest mistakes we can make in evangelism is to rely on our own understanding and power. Passages like 1 Corinthians 2:9 and Ephesians 3:20 show us that this is futile because God is so far beyond even our wildest imaginations. Our eyes have not seen, nor our ears heard what He has in store for us because He can provide far more abundantly than we can ask of Him. The Holy Spirit inspired Paul to write these passages, in part, to establish that we are finite beings with a limited ability to understand. It is only through God, the infinite one who goes far beyond our finite capacities, that we are able to find true peace. The greatest spiritual minds on the planet cannot compete.

I doubt most Christians would question that the peace that passes understanding comes only from God. The problem is not that we question its origin, but that we don't quite know how to attain it. I believe that the very foundation for us attaining a relationship with God is through Jesus and on His terms. Anything else is immaterial in regards to eternity.

One of the many powerful passages to aid our understanding of this God-designed relationship is Matthew 11:28-30:

> Come unto me all you who labor and are heavy laden, and I will give you rest. Take my yoke upon you and learn of me for I am meek and lowly in heart and you shall find rest to your souls. For my yoke is easy and my burden is light.

I have spoken with many lost souls who struggle with the idea that Jesus promises persecution to those who follow Him. They ask, "How can that possibly be a light burden or an easy yoke?" To understand this properly, one needs a knowledge of the two possible spiritual states. Outside of Jesus a person incurs the penalty for breaking the spiritual law from the throne of God: "You sin, you die." Inside of Jesus (yoked with Him) the burden is light and the yoke is easy because this is where faithful Christians are continually forgiven. If one sins outside of Jesus there is no forgiveness, even if that heart is changed and dedicated to never committing that same sin again. The penalty for the first sin has not been remitted, and never doing it again cannot remove the sin already committed. The ledger has a blot that a million good works can never remove. In contrast, the Christian will continue to sin as well, but their ledger of life is continually wiped clean by the blood of Jesus. The better choice is clear.

This choice requires movement on our part as Jesus calls "come to Me." Those who are qualified to come are the ones who labor and are heavy laden. He does not desire that sluggards and the idle come to Him because he cannot cause growth within an unwilling or lazy spirit. He certainly wants them to repent and respond, but has no use for a person in that state of mind.

And so it makes sense that he says if you labor and are heavy laden, He will give you rest. In the original Greek, the word "rest" is "anapowoo," which means to give repose or refreshing. This isn't the same as plopping into the recliner after a hard day's work. Instead, Jesus offers rest in our work. This type of rest leads us to a peace that passes understanding, an inner peace that propels us to operate even in the face of danger and persecution.

Another requirement to obtaining this rest is to take up Jesus' yoke—quite a strange statement at first glance but powerful when understood correctly. The word "yoke" literally means a "beam of balancing" and has to do with coupling two things together. We need to be coupled to the Savior in order to find balance in our lives, which includes the absence of guilt and the comfort of forgiveness and guidance. There is another interesting insight given us here with the use of the word "upon." In Greek, this word is "epi" and gives the idea of superimposing. His yoke, when superimposed upon us, leads to self-satisfaction and peace.

A farmer would yoke a young ox to an older one for the purpose of training the young ox to follow the older one. Applied spiritually, Jesus is the strong ox and we are the youth that needs His guidance. How many times have we abandoned the wisdom from above and tried to do things our way, only to find ourselves needing to be reunited to Jesus in His yoke?

In the wonderfully expressive Greek language, He continues to identify the end process with another form of the word "rest" used earlier. This word is "anapousis," which involves the idea of recreation. How perfect is this analogy to get the idea across to us as we labor? Jesus is telling us that if we yoke with Him, we will begin to discover the peace only He can provide as we labor in this endeavor.

We should also read between the lines to notice what He did not say to us. He never said discomfort, division, opposition, persecution, or difficulty will be removed from our lives. In fact, He says the opposite is true (Matthew 10:22). Due to this, the Holy Spirit went to great lengths to warn and advise us on the territory, the wisdom to navigate it, the need for yoking with Him, the growth process, and the peacefulness available to us as we evangelize.

Practical Applications

This book nearly made it to print without this chapter. Thankfully, the encouragement of a dear brother from Texas caused me to examine the material more closely from the perspective of a potential reader. I had described the role of the Bringer but had failed to ask how the information could be applied in a practical sense. And so, in this section, you'll find a number of everyday scenarios with ideas on how to reach out to people without relying on ineffective evangelistic practices (repetition of canned phrases, failing to meet people where they are at, fire and brimstone condemnation, etc.). I want to help you think about your unique situation and how you can use your God-given traits and abilities to share the Gospel with others.

BLOOMING WHERE WE'RE PLANTED

Earlier in the book, we talked about how a mother with small children could use her station in life as an opportunity to share the Gospel. Let's look at a couple more examples of how common situations can be used to reach others.

A Business Owner

I owned a lawn service for many years and worked hard to set myself apart from the competition in order to generate not only business, but also Bible studies with my customers. What could I provide that others in the business did not? The answer was the spirit of my staff and the quality of our workmanship, which I cultivated with intentionality and seriousness. Here are a few of the things I instituted to subtly reflect Jesus through my company:

1. Every employee was to wear long pants and a company provided shirt and hat, which served two purposes. It reflected a sense of professionalism and immediately identified them with my business.

2. Language was to be gracious at all times whether the customer was gracious or not. Obviously, foul or abrasive language was unacceptable.

3. If it was garbage pickup day, my employees were required to bring the garbage cans back up to the front of the house. This was an extra touch that helped us stand out as being relationship-conscious. Our customers loved it.

4. We would carefully blow the cobwebs off of the porch lights, make sure the driveway cracks were free of clippings, and clean off children's slides and swings. We would walk up on their deck and blow it clear of leaves, even if we didn't put any grass clippings up there. These were all extras that made a very good impression.

Although these things cost us some time and money up front, they actually paid off big in the long run. Our prices could be a bit higher than the competition because our customers loved working with our staff. The relationships we developed allowed us to make mistakes and still retain our customers as long as we fixed or apologized for those mistakes. In the end, I ran a successful business and my attempts to reflect Jesus translated into Bible studies.

Do you own a business? Think about how you represent yourself to the employees who are not Christians and then to your customers. What could you do to improve?

An Employee

Most of us have been employees at some point in our lives, so it's not difficult to come up with a list of ways to show Christ-like behavior in this role. Things like work effort, punctuality, language, and quality of work all come to mind. While these are the basics that every employee has a responsibility to provide, the Christian should do them with an above-and-beyond level of excellence. The key is an attitude of thankfulness to God for providing employment. Consider the following:

1. How do you talk about your employment with others, including fellow employees, family, and friends. Luke 6:45 states that, "Out of the abundance of the heart, the mouth speaks. Evil hearts produce evil and good hearts produce good." It is fine to talk about some negative aspects of your job; however, your speech should never belie the thankfulness you show to God.

2. If you are representing your heart to others as being unthankful for the job you have, are you seeking out another one to replace it? The key is to be thankful for the job you have while seeing if there is another one that would provide a better

environment for you.

3. What is the tone in your voice towards your supervisors? Many of us have worked under folks that have been terrible leaders. Have you tried to help them? Have you taken them aside and given advice on areas you may better grasp? Or have you said "yes" to their face and then complained to other employees about them?

Even in these tough situations, God provides an opportunity for us to be an example to those who are seeking. A light shines much brighter in darkness!

A Customer

In our society, we are all customers in one way or another. As we purchase goods and services, we have an opportunity to reach out to others. Imagine your favorite restaurant as the setting for our next hypothetical scenario. How do you treat the server when you sit down to order a meal? Do you behave as if they are your slave or as a person that Jesus gave His life for? I'm ashamed to say that I have seen Christians lash out at servers for messing up an order or burning the coffee. It's an absolute disgrace to our Lord to prioritize the condition of a meal over the soul of another human being.

Let me share an incredible experience Michelle and I had on the way home from a seminar in 2016. Tired and hungry from the long trip, we stopped one night at a local steakhouse to get dinner. This particular restaurant was split into different tiers, some higher in elevation than others, and our table was on the highest level. From this vantage point, we could clearly see everyone in the establishment, including a family of 8 seated down the main aisle. This large family consisted of mom, dad, and 6 children, ranging from about 3 to 13 years of age. About halfway into our meal, we witnessed the waitress spill a glass of ice water on the young man at the end of the table as she tried to squeeze behind his chair. The youngster sat straight up in his chair with a look of utter shock in his face. The waitress hurriedly gathered towels to dry the young man off while apologizing profusely.

Stop for a moment and consider what you would have done in that situation. Also consider how you believe most other people would respond. Here's what the parents did. The mom softly said to the waitress, "It's OK, he will be just fine. Please don't worry about it." The dad turned to the son and said, "You're fine, right? If you need to be warmed up you can have my jacket." The incredible display of tact and forgiveness left an impression on us that we won't soon forget.

And here's what the parents didn't do. They did not ask to see the manager, complain and raise a fuss, ask for free meals, walk out of the restaurant, or chastise the waitress. Instead, they actually comforted her! I was so touched that when we left, I stopped at the table and commended the young man on how he handled the situation. I then said to the parents, "Whatever you are doing to raise such a wonderful family, keep it up!"

As "Bringers," we must be aware that when we are out and about, our actions leave an impression on those around us. We are always being watched. I encourage you—through self-evaluation and the critique of others—to think about changes you can make to positively affect those around you. Let's make sure that we let our lights shine so we give others a chance to "see our good works and glorify our Father in Heaven" (Matt. 5:16).

Grandparents

My wife and I enjoy a wonderful relationship with our grand-daughter. We are blessed with a faithful daughter and son-in-law, so it is easy for us to have a positive influence on her. We support the principles of child raising that they employ, making sure when we are alone with her to reinforce the responsibility she has to listen to and obey her parents.

However, many Christians have children and grandchildren who are not faithful, which creates a totally different dynamic. Take any opportunity to use what I refer to as "the grandparent card." The relationship you build with them while they are being raised will often determine if they will listen to you when they are older. Simple statements such as, "Honey, it would make grandma and grandpa so happy if you would come and worship with us next Sunday" can make all the difference in the world. Should they come, make sure to introduce them to a lot of brethren, especially those their age. Grandparents often have tremendous influence on grandchildren which can lead them to spiritual safety.

DEALING WITH AN UGLY ATTITUDE

Our ministry has taken us throughout many parts of the United States. As we've travelled, we've noticed a consistent lack of knowledge about the Biblical plan of evangelism, especially regarding the roles of the Brother's Keeper and Bringer. If the church is to fulfill Jesus' commission, the ignorance about evangelism cannot continue. But even more so, we've encountered a more damaging ugliness that threatens to undermine even the most well prepared of us all: an unloving attitude.

Congregations in some areas have made it very clear to their community that they see themselves as the "Sin Police." They don't wear special badges or promote it on the sign out front, but the attitude of their members and approach to those in the community make it obvious. I hear it from group sessions when I travel and hold discussions on bringing. The content of the message they take to the community is usually summed up like so: "You are going to Hell if you aren't a member of the church of Christ."

Let me take this opportunity to be very clear of my stance. In John 14:6, Jesus says, "I am the Way, the Truth and the Life and no one comes to the Father except by Me." This means that anyone who is not "in Christ" will not make it to Heaven. Any who follow a doctrine, sect, or religion other than the one Jesus established are not saved unless they repent. I don't believe this is too harsh a concept for anyone who reads the Bible and studies it with a seeking heart. The problem is that we too often take this message of salvation out to those in such a way that violates the wisdom of Mark 4:33: "Jesus taught as they were able to bear."

Let me illustrate it this way. Would you walk up to an overweight person and say, "You sure are fat!" What type of reaction would you expect to get from them? That isn't being truthful, it's just plain mean (even if it is the truth). Wouldn't it be better to befriend the person and encourage them to become healthier? This principle needs to be applied to how we share the Gospel with others. We need to be encouragers, not condemners. Let's learn to speak "as others are able to bear!"

KNOWING THE BOOK

There is another epidemic in the church that crosses all state lines. We usually describe it as a general lack of Bible knowledge and there is a lot of truth to that statement. However, I believe it goes a bit further to not understanding the "structure" of the Book. Long ago I was given a bookmark that divides the Old Testament books into 5 categories: Law, History, Wisdom (Poetry), Major Prophets, and Minor Prophets. At that point in my spiritual life, I dismissed these designations because I didn't understand the reason we should know them that way. Recently, I asked my Sunday class why it might be important to group them this way. The vast majority just learned the information that morning, so they had no idea how to respond. So why is it important?

Unbeknownst to many, an evil has infiltrated the church where some prominent leaders have begun to dismiss the first 11 chapters of Genesis as poetry. In other words, they view them as metaphorical and not historical. The problem is that Hebrew poets used parallelism and imagery heavily in their works and the first 11 chapters of Genesis do not include these features, disqualifying them as poetry. Additionally, if we interpret these 11 chapters as metaphor then our Savior is the descendant of a metaphor. This is preposterous. I hope you can see why it's vital for Christians to understand the structure of the Bible.

The deprioritization of memory work for adults is another big problem in the modern church. We commonly teach our young children to memorize the books of the Bible, the names of the Apostles, and the 12 tribes of Israel. Now walk into any adult class, ask the same questions, and observe the reaction. Faces point downward, hoping to escape embarrassment. Are we teaching our children that it is beneficial for them but not important enough to remember as they grow older? We are supposed to be people of the book, and yet we fail to have in memory these very basics.

You may be asking yourself why I include items like this in a book about bringing, when these concepts seem to be most important in the area of teaching. Not only are these important to our personal faith, they give us confidence in reaching out to others. Do not conclude that I am suggesting you wait until you acquire all of this knowledge before you reach out to folks. There is no certification or test involved. My encouragement is to begin from where you are and work accordingly.

1. For those with a solid grasp of the structure of the Bible:

If you're in this category, the advantage you have in reaching out to people is that you may be able to educate folks who do not know these things. Being able to share the structure of the Bible with someone can establish trust and generate interest. During this discussion you may be able to say something like, "I know someone who knows a lot about these things and has taught me a lot. If you'd like to be in on our studies I know he'd welcome you." This "entire body working in evangelism" concept takes the responsibility to teach people off of the shoulders of the bringers. They can focus on the best way to get them to the teacher.

2. For those who do not grasp the structure of the Bible yet:

The first piece of advice and encouragement I can give is to be intentional about learning more and becoming as knowledgeable as possible. Knowing more about the structure of the Bible will only make you a better bringer. In the meantime, one of the best ways that you can reach out is to invite others to study with a teacher from your congregation. Always think about where the invitation would have the best chance of a "yes" response and ask something like this:

Christian: "Bob, have you ever studied the Bible?"

Bob: "I hear a lot about it but have never looked into it."

Christian: "I was in the same boat until a friend invited me to a study where a guy did a timeline of the Bible. It actually opened my eyes to a lot of things I didn't know. It was really more than I expected. If you ever want to see it, let me know. He does them all the time."

Note that there was no hint of condemnation in the Christian's approach. The offer to Bob was very gentle and non-threatening, which gave him the opportunity to respond however he wished. He was not forced into a defensive position. If seeking, Bob would jump at the chance to study. If not, at least he was given a very nice offer with no sign of the "sin police" present.

Now suppose Bob answered very roughly by saying, "You Bible thumpers think you have all the answers. What, I'm not a good person? You think you have all of life's answers for me because of that book you read and try to cram down my throat! I hate when you guys act like that!" The Christian's answer would be a bit different than in the above scenario, but could be delivered with the same sentiment. In response, he could say, "Man, I don't blame you. I hate that too! I had a guy show me a timeline of the Bible and it helped me. I just wanted to share it with you too. If you change your mind just let me know."

In the last 30 years of evangelism ministry, I have seldom encountered a rejection that harsh because I didn't just go out swinging; Instead, I prayed for wisdom to navigate the territory. I have been shunned, persecuted, laughed at, and even lost employment, but rarely received a blistering response because I learned to be wiser as I spoke to people.

Please take these thoughts as they are intended: to encourage you to allow the God of Heaven to providentially develop you as you strive to get His Gospel message to the world. Remember that as Christians we are different, having been sanctified to a holiness without which no one can see God (Hebrews 12:14). This passage in Hebrews goes on to say that Esau shirked his responsibility as the firstborn and heir by selling his birthright for a plate of beans. He was to carry on the honored name of his father, but instead disgraced his family and insulted God. It is so easy to make excuses and refuse to grow once we reach a certain age. When we do this, we sell out just like Esau did.

Listen to the words of the Holy Spirit given to us through Paul in Ephesians 3:20- 21: "Now to Him who is able to do far more abundantly than all that we ask or think, according to the power at work within us, to Him be the glory in the church and in Christ Jesus throughout all generations, forever and ever, Amen!" Understand it, believe it, and strive to live it, then brace yourself for what God will do through you!

THE WORD, NOT THE WORLD.

At the time of this writing, in August 2017, so much is happening in the world to produce uncertainty and division. The first year of the Donald Trump presidency has evoked a venomous hatred that I have not seen in my 60 years of life. Fear over a possible nuclear stand-off has captivated the attention of the world, while moral standards are being eroded at an unprecedented rate. As a society, we cannot figure out which bathroom to use, what gender we are, or what marriage is all about. On top of that, you go to jail for kicking a dog but can easily obtain financing to kill your unborn child. Lines are being drawn and the rift between political parties continues to widen.

Sadly, I'm hearing many Christians talk as if one's political alignment is grounds for disfellowship. I actually had one person say to me, "You seated me next to a Democrat" when I laid out seating assignments in a class a few years ago. "No," I retorted, "I sat you next to your sister in Christ." God condemns this kind of disunity in His family! Paul's words in 1 Corinthians 3 ring just as true today as they did when they were first written: "I could not address you as spiritual people, but people of the flesh." Always remember, we will not be judged upon our political affiliation but upon our faithfulness to Jesus. There is sufficient error in all lines of human thinking, so instead, let's align our thoughts with the One who knows no error in His leadership.

I see a huge opportunity for Christians as the world continues to wage its war on God-honored principles and values. Truly, a light shines brighter in the darkness. We are different and this is good. That's why I'm so proud of the unity at my home congregation, the church of Christ in Waterford, MI. We honor New Testament worship. We offer an invitation that encourages those who need help to come forward and be assured they are in a "judgment free" zone. We share our drug, alcohol, and marriage issues with each other, knowing that we will not be avoided but embraced. This is valuable for us who need help, but it also shows our visitors that we don't intend to shoot our wounded. The world cannot offer this to them! Only God can. So don't be dismayed by the state of the territory. Instead, be emboldened to dedicate yourself to a life in Jesus that relies on His power, His guidance, His forgiveness and His promise to those who remain faithful—a crown of life that only He, the righteous judge, will give you (2 Timothy 4:7-8). May we honor our God by committing to the cause for which He laid hold of us!

Conclusion

If you were unsure about your role as a bringer, I hope that this book has solidified your conviction one way or the other. As you continue to grow in one or more of the 3 areas of evangelism, seek God's will for your life in prayer, ask other Christians for wisdom, and hone your craft through practice. Think about the individuals in your life and how you can approach them with the Gospel. You may want to start out simple by throwing a small get-together at your place and asking both Christian and non-Christian friends to come. Let your worldly friends be influenced for good and build relationships with other Christians. If the opportunity presents itself, invite someone to a study or church service. Above all, put on a heart of love because "perfect love casts out fear" (1 John 4:18a).

Your role as a bringer is critical for the whole model of evangelism to operate efficiently. It is exciting to know that when you reach out to others there is a group of teachers within the church who are willing to study further with those individuals. And if those seekers eventually become Christians, it is reassuring to know that there is a system set up to continually surround them with friends and materials that will prepare them for their eternal reward. It sure beats offering the Gospel to a friend and having no idea what the next step will be for him!

Made in the USA
Middletown, DE
26 September 2023